Title.

Mastering Scikit-Learn: A Journey into Machine

Learning with Python

Table of *of* Contents:

Chapter 1: The Odyssey Begins

- Introduction to Machine Learning
- Python's Role in ML
- Welcoming Scikit-Learn

Chapter 2: Meet the Cast

- Characters: Decision Trees, Random Forests, SVMs, K-Means, and more
- Understanding the Ensemble: Bagging and Boosting
- The Power of Neural Networks

Chapter 3: The Prelude to Code

- Setting Up Your Environment
- Installing Scikit-Learn
- The Pythonic Way: Importing Libraries

Chapter 4: Unveiling the Datasets

- Famous Faces: Iris, Digits, and Wine
- Real-world Datasets: Challenges and Opportunities
- The Art of Data Exploration

Chapter 5: The Dance of Preprocessing

- Cleaning the Stage: Handling Missing Data
- The Ensemble's Harmony: Feature Scaling and Normalization
- One-Hot Encoders and Label Encoders: Decoding the Ciphers

Chapter 6: Crafting the First Model

- Supervised Learning: A Gentle Start
- Linear Regression: Predicting the Future

- *Decision Trees: The Art of Choices*

Chapter 7: Navigating the Model Landscape

- *Random Forests: The Collaborative Ensemble*
- *Support Vector Machines: Finding the Hyperplane*
- *K-Nearest Neighbors: Birds of a Feather*

Chapter 8: The Validation Waltz

- *Splitting the Stage: Train-Test Split*
- *Cross-Validation: The Art of Learning from Every Step*
- *Grid Search: Finding the Optimal Footwork*

Chapter 9: The Clustering Chronicles

- *Unsupervised Learning: A Tale of Discovery*
- *K-Means: The Quest for Centers*
- *Hierarchical Clustering: The Family Tree*

Chapter 10: The Deep Learning Saga

- *Neural Networks: An Introduction*
- *Keras: A Symphony of Deep Learning*
- *Convolutional Neural Networks (CNNs): Images Speak Louder*

Chapter 11: The Grand Finale

- *Model Evaluation Metrics: Bowing to Accuracy, Precision, and Recall*
- *Overfitting and Underfitting: The Traps of the Performance Stage*
- *Deploying Models: From Rehearsal to the Live Performance*

Chapter 12: Epilogue

- *The Future of Scikit-Learn*
- *The Ongoing Machine Learning Odyssey*
- *Acknowledgments and References*

Appendix: The Script of Code

- Code snippets and examples from each chapter

This fictional outline combines the technical journey of learning scikit-learn with a storytelling approach, making it engaging for readers. Each chapter introduces new characters (machine learning algorithms), builds a plot (learning concepts), and provides examples and dialogue (code snippets) for hands-on learning. The goal is to make the book not only informative but also an enjoyable read for those venturing into the world of scikit-learn.

Chapter 1:

The Odyssey Begins

Setting: A cozy study room with a computer, where our protagonist, Alex, is embarking on a journey into the fascinating world of Machine Learning.

Narrator: *In a small town, under the glow of a desk lamp, Alex sat down, eager to unravel the secrets of Machine Learning. Little did Alex know that this journey would take them to uncharted territories of algorithms, predictions, and the heart of Python itself.*

Alex: *(excitedly)* "Alright, here we go. Machine Learning – the term sounds intriguing. But what is it really?"

Mentor Python: *(appearing on the screen)* "Ah, Alex! Welcome to the realm of possibilities. Machine Learning is like having a digital crystal ball. It's about training computers to learn from data and make predictions or decisions without being explicitly programmed."

Alex: "So, Python is the key to unlocking this mystical world?"

Mentor Python: "Absolutely! Python is the wizard's wand here. Its simplicity and vast libraries make it a go-to language for Machine Learning. And guess what? Scikit-Learn is our magical toolkit within Python."

Alex: (curious) "Tell me more about this Scikit-Learn. What makes it special?"

Mentor Python: "Scikit-Learn is like a wise old mentor in our journey. It provides a simple and efficient tool for data analysis and modeling. It's open-source, built on NumPy, SciPy, and Matplotlib – our loyal companions in this adventure."

Alex: "Interesting. But where do we start?"

Mentor Python: "Let's dive in, Alex. First, understand the types of Machine Learning: supervised, unsupervised, and reinforcement learning. It's like learning to ride a bicycle, but the bike learns from you!"

Alex: *(nodding)* "Got it. And how does supervised learning work?"

Mentor Python: *"Picture this: you're a teacher, and your computer is the student. You show it examples, labeled with the correct answers. The computer learns to make predictions based on these examples. It's the heart of tasks like regression and classification."*

Alex: "Fascinating! And what about unsupervised learning?"

Mentor Python: *"Ah, unsupervised learning is like a mystery novel. You give the computer a bunch of data without labels, and it discovers the patterns and relationships on its own. Clustering and dimensionality reduction are its tools of choice."*

Alex: *(intrigued)* "I'm hooked! And reinforcement learning?"

Mentor Python: *"Think of it as training a pet. The computer learns by trial and error, receiving feedback in the form of rewards or punishments. It's how AI learns to play games and make decisions."*

Alex: *"This is incredible! I can't wait to explore more. What's next?"*

Mentor Python: *"Next, my eager learner, we'll delve into the Pythonic ways of preparing for this journey. Buckle up, Alex – the real adventure is about to begin!"*

As the screen flickers, Alex eagerly opens the Python terminal, ready for the first steps into the enchanting world of Machine Learning with Scikit-Learn.

Chapter 2:

Meet the Cast

Setting: *The Python terminal, where Alex is greeted by a lively group of characters – Decision Trees, Random Forests, SVMs, K-Means, and more.*

Narrator: *In the digital kingdom of Python, our protagonist Alex found themselves surrounded by an ensemble of characters, each with its unique charm and role to play in the grand Machine Learning narrative.*

Alex: *(excited)* *"Wow, this is quite the cast of characters! Who are these Decision Trees, Random Forests, SVMs, and K-Means I've been hearing about?"*

Decision Tree: *(raising a leafy branch)* *"Greetings, Alex! I am Decision Tree, a versatile algorithm that loves making decisions by branching out, just like a flowchart. I'm perfect for both classification and regression tasks."*

Random Forest: *(swaying with enthusiasm)* "And I'm Random Forest, a collection of Decision Trees working together like a wise council. We reduce overfitting and bring stability to predictions."

SVM: *(standing tall)* "Salutations, Alex. I am Support Vector Machine, skilled in finding the best hyperplane to separate data points. My expertise lies in both linear and non-linear classifications."

K-Means: *(with open arms)* "Hello, Alex! I am K-Means, the clustering maestro. I group similar data points together, creating a harmonious dance of patterns."

Neural Network: *(emerging with a spark)* "And I am the Neural Network, a network of interconnected nodes inspired by the human brain. My power lies in complex tasks like image recognition and natural language processing."

Alex: *(amazed)* "It's like assembling a dream team! But what's this talk about Ensemble, Bagging, and Boosting?"

Ensemble: (stepping forward) "Ah, Ensemble is the secret sauce, Alex! It's the art of combining the strengths of different models to create a supermodel. Bagging and Boosting are our magical spells to enhance performance."

Bagging: (waving a bag) "I'm Bagging, short for Bootstrap Aggregating. I create diverse subsets of data, train models separately, and then blend their wisdom for robust predictions."

Boosting: (shouting with energy) "And I am Boosting! I boost the confidence of weaker models by giving them a chance to learn from their mistakes. Together, we rise stronger!"

Alex: "This is fascinating! But Neural Networks seem like the rockstars of this ensemble. What's their power, really?"

Neural Network: "Think of me as a master musician conducting an orchestra. I can learn intricate patterns, adapt to complex scenarios, and unveil the magic behind tasks that seem impossible for other algorithms."

Alex: *(intrigued) "I want to see this magic in action! Can we explore an example?"*

Narrator: *And so, our adventure continues as Alex, along with this diverse cast of characters, begins to explore the enchanting world of Decision Trees, Random Forests, SVMs, K-Means, and the powerful Neural Networks. Little did they know that each character had a unique story to tell, and together, they would create a symphony of machine intelligence.*

As the Python code unfolds on the screen, Alex immerses themselves in the realm of algorithms, eager to witness the magic that unfolds.

Chapter 3:

The Prelude to Code

Setting: A cozy virtual coding den where Alex is guided by an enthusiastic mentor, Pythona.

Narrator: *In the heart of Pythonland, Alex found themselves in a virtual coding den, ready to embark on a journey into the realm of Scikit-Learn. The wise mentor, Pythona, was there to guide them through the prelude to the enchanting world of code.*

Pythona: *(smiling)* "Welcome, Alex! Before we dive into the magical world of Scikit-Learn, let's ensure your coding den is set up for the adventure. Have you installed Python?"

Alex: *(nodding)* "Yes, Python is my trusty sidekick. Ready to roll!"

Pythona: "Excellent! Now, let's invite Scikit-Learn to join our party. Open your command console and type 'pip install scikit-learn'."

Alex: (typing away) "Installing the magic potion, Scikit-Learn, as we speak. What's next?"

Pythona: "Great! Now, imagine libraries as spells in your wizard's book. We need to import them to cast our code spells. Let's start with the basics. Type 'import numpy as np' to bring the power of numerical computing."

Alex: (typing) "Got it. numpy is now my magical wand, and np is the incantation. What's next?"

Pythona: "Good job, Alex! Now, let's summon pandas, the mystical data manipulation library. 'import pandas as pd' will do the trick."

Alex: (enthused) "pandas, the data sorcerer! I'm ready to explore the realms of data frames. What's next on our spellbook?"

Pythona: *"Now, let's welcome Matplotlib, the visualization wizard. 'import matplotlib.pyplot as plt' will bring art to our data journey."*

Alex: *(feeling the magic) "Matplotlib, the artist! Our plots will be masterpieces. What else do we need, Pythona?"*

Pythona: *"To complete our party, let's invite Seaborn, the stylish plot enhancer. 'import seaborn as sns' will add elegance to our visual spells."*

Alex: *(smiling) "Seaborn, the style guru! Our plots will be the talk of the town. Anything else, Pythona?"*

Pythona: *"For now, that's a solid foundation. With NumPy, pandas, Matplotlib, and Seaborn by your side, you're armed to face any data challenge. Now, let's brew some code potions and witness the magic!"*

Narrator: As the code den filled with the whispers of spellbound libraries, Alex and Pythona began crafting the first lines of code. Little did Alex know that this prelude was just the beginning of a captivating coding odyssey.

The Python console lit up with each import statement, setting the stage for the magic to unfold.

Chapter 4:

Unveiling
the Datasets

Setting: *The coding den, adorned with datasets and a sense of anticipation. Alex and Pythona prepare for the grand reveal.*

Narrator: *In the luminous coding den, Alex and Pythona stood surrounded by datasets, each holding a tale waiting to be uncovered.*

Alex: *(curious)* *"What datasets do we have in this mystical realm, Pythona?"*

Pythona: *(smirking)* *"Ah, Alex, prepare to meet the famous faces of the machine learning world. First up, the Iris dataset."*

Alex: *(intrigued)* *"Iris? Like the flower?"*

Pythona: "Exactly! It contains measurements of iris flowers—petal length, petal width, sepal length, and sepal width. A classic tale in the ML saga."

Alex: (nodding) "Fascinating! What other legends await us?"

Pythona: "Next, we have Digits, a collection of handwritten digits. Perfect for those who seek to decipher the ancient art of digit recognition."

Alex: (smiling) "Digits, the storytellers of handwritten wisdom. And the third legend?"

Pythona: "Behold, the Wine dataset! A connoisseur's delight, featuring wine characteristics. Red or white, it holds the secrets of flavor and aroma."

Alex: (enthused) "Wine, the elixir of data exploration! These datasets have a charm of their own. But what about real-world challenges?"

Pythona: *(leaning in)* "Ah, real-world datasets—a realm filled with challenges and opportunities. Imagine datasets like housing prices, customer reviews, or weather patterns. They bring a touch of unpredictability and real-world magic to our journey."

Alex: *(pensively)* "So, Pythona, how do we begin unraveling these tales?"

Pythona: "With the art of data exploration, my apprentice. We'll summon pandas to manipulate and seaborn to visualize. Let's load the Iris dataset and see the magic unfold."

Alex: *(eagerly)* "I'm ready! Show me the first lines of this data saga."

Pythona: "Type 'import seaborn as sns' to summon the visualization powers. Then, 'sns.load_dataset("iris")' to bring the Iris dataset into our realm."

Alex: *(typing away) "Seaborn, unveil the Iris dataset!"*

Narrator: *As the code echoed in the den, the Iris dataset materialized before them. Petals and sepals danced in a symphony of data. Little did Alex know that this was just the beginning of their exploration into the vast realms of datasets.*

And so, with each dataset unveiled, Alex and Pythona continued their journey, discovering the tales hidden within the rows and columns of data.

Stay tuned for the next chapter, where Alex and Pythona dive deeper into the enchanting world of data exploration.

Chapter 5:

The Dance of Pre-Processing

Setting: *The preprocessing ballroom, adorned with missing values and encoding masks. Alex and Pythona prepare for the dance of data preparation.*

Narrator: *In the preprocessing ballroom, where missing data and encoded ciphers awaited their turn to shine, Alex and Pythona readied themselves for the dance of data preparation.*

Alex: *(examining the stage)* "This ballroom is quite mysterious, Pythona. What do we have in store for today's dance?"

Pythona: *(with a twirl)* "Today, my dear Alex, we embark on the noble quest of cleaning the stage. Missing data, the hidden villain, must be vanquished first."

Alex: *(raising an eyebrow)* "Missing data, a villain? What harm does it cause?"

Pythona: *"Imagine a dance with incomplete partners—missing data creates gaps in our story. We must fill these gaps gracefully. Let's start with the Iris dataset."*

Alex: *(ready to code)* *"Seaborn, Iris dataset, and missing data—let the dance begin!"*

Pythona: *"First, call 'sns.heatmap(df.isnull(), cbar=False, cmap='viridis')' to visualize the missing data. Identify the gaps in our dance floor."*

Alex: *(typing away)* *"Heatmap, reveal the missing beats!"*

Narrator: *As the heatmap unfolded, missing beats in the Iris dataset became apparent. A dance floor speckled with gaps awaited their attention.*

Pythona: *"Now, Alex, we shall gracefully fill these gaps. Use 'df.dropna()' to discard rows with missing data or 'df.fillna(value)' to fill them with a chosen value."*

Alex: *(choosing his move) "Filling the gaps with dance partners or gracefully removing them. Got it!"*

Pythona: *"Next, the ensemble's harmony—feature scaling and normalization. Our dancers must move in unison, regardless of their scales. Use 'MinMaxScaler' to bring them into harmony."*

Alex: *(excited) "MinMaxScaler, the choreographer for our ensemble!"*

Pythona: *"And now, the grand finale—encoding our dancers. One-Hot Encoders and Label Encoders shall decode the ciphers, transforming categorical features into a language the ensemble understands."*

Alex: *(intrigued) "Decoding ciphers? I'm eager to see this transformation!"*

Pythona: *"For categorical columns, use 'pd.get_dummies(df, columns=['categorical_column'])' for One-Hot Encoding or 'LabelEncoder' for ordinal categories."*

Alex: *(enchanting the data) "One-Hot Encoders and Label Encoders, reveal the hidden meanings within!"*

Narrator: *As the dance of preprocessing unfolded, missing beats were restored, and the ensemble harmonized. The encoded ciphers whispered tales of transformation, and the stage was set for the grand performance of machine learning.*

Stay tuned for the next chapter, where Alex and Pythona take their prepared dataset to the training arena.

Chapter 6:

Crafting the First Model

Setting: *The model crafting workshop, adorned with algorithms and predictions. Alex and Pythona embark on the journey of building their first models.*

Narrator: *In the model crafting workshop, where algorithms awaited their turn to shine, Alex and Pythona prepared to embark on the journey of crafting their first models.*

Alex: *(surveying the workshop)* "So many algorithms to choose from, Pythona. Where do we begin our modeling adventure?"

Pythona: *(with a knowing smile)* "Let's start with the gentle embrace of supervised learning. Linear Regression shall be our guide—a simple, yet powerful, way to predict the future."

Alex: *(intrigued)* "Predicting the future? That sounds magical!"

Pythona: *"Magical indeed! Picture this: a linear relationship between features and outcomes. We use this relationship to predict future outcomes. First, load your dataset and split it into training and testing sets."*

Alex: *(ready to code) "Loading the dataset, splitting the stage. Onward!"*

Narrator: *As the dataset took its place on the stage, Alex and Pythona prepared for the first act of their modeling adventure.*

Pythona: *"Now, summon the magic of Linear Regression. Use 'from sklearn.linear_model import LinearRegression' to bring our guide into the scene."*

Alex: *(conjuring the magic) "Linear Regression, enter the stage!"*

Pythona: *"Prepare the X_train, X_test, y_train, and y_test ensemble. Fit the model with 'model.fit(X_train, y_train)' to let it learn the dance moves."*

Alex: *(orchestrating the training) "Fit the model, let the dance of learning begin!"*

Narrator: *The Linear Regression model embraced the dance of learning, adjusting its parameters to the rhythm of the training data.*

Pythona: *"Ah, the model has learned its steps. Now, let's see it dance on the test stage. Predict outcomes with 'y_pred = model.predict(X_test)'."*

Alex: *(eagerly) "Prediction time! Let's unveil the future!"*

Pythona: *"Visualize the predictions alongside the actual outcomes. A plot, my dear Alex, is worth a thousand words."*

Alex: *(summoning matplotlib) "Behold, the plot unfolds!"*

Narrator: *As the plot unfolded, the Linear Regression model showcased its predictive prowess. But the modeling adventure was far from over.*

Pythona: *"Now, let's introduce another character: Decision Trees. An artist of choices, Decision Trees craft a path based on features, leading to unique outcomes."*

Alex: *(curious) "Choices and outcomes? That sounds fascinating!"*

Pythona: *"Load 'DecisionTreeRegressor' from sklearn.tree. Fit the model, predict outcomes, and witness the branching choices."*

Alex: *(ready for the second act)* *"Decision Tree, take the stage! Fit, predict, and show us your choices!"*

Narrator: *The Decision Tree model took its place, crafting a path through the features and revealing its unique choices.*

Pythona: *"Our first models have danced beautifully on the stage of supervised learning. Linear Regression predicts with grace, and Decision Trees make choices like artists. The adventure continues—stay tuned for the next chapter, where we delve deeper into the world of algorithms."*

To be continued...

Chapter 7:

Navigating the Model Landscape

Setting: *The Model Landscape, where algorithms gathered for a grand summit. Alex and Pythona explore the terrain of Random Forests, Support Vector Machines, and K-Nearest Neighbors.*

Narrator: *In the vast expanse of the Model Landscape, where algorithms gathered like attendees at a grand summit, Alex and Pythona embarked on a quest to explore the terrain.*

Alex: *(surveying the landscape)* "So many models, each with its unique character. Where shall we venture next, Pythona?"

Pythona: *(pointing to a lively group of models)* "Behold, the Collaborative Ensemble known as Random Forests. A group of decision trees working together, each contributing its wisdom to make predictions."

Alex: *(intrigued)* *"Collaborative decision trees? That sounds like a powerful ensemble. How do we summon this forest?"*

Pythona: *"Fear not, Alex. Import 'RandomForestRegressor' from sklearn. Prepare your dataset and split it. Just like with Linear Regression and Decision Trees, fit the model and unveil the collective predictions."*

Alex: *(preparing to code)* *"Random Forests, assemble! Let the collaborative predictions begin!"*

Narrator: *As the Random Forests ensemble assembled, decision trees collaborated to craft predictions, showcasing the strength of unity.*

Pythona: *"Now, let's embark on a quest to find the mighty Hyperplane with Support Vector Machines. Import 'SVR' from sklearn.svm and prepare for a journey into the realm of hyperplanes."*

Alex: (ready for the journey) "Support Vector Machines, guide us to the realm of hyperplanes! Fit the model, predict outcomes, and let the hyperplane unfold."

Narrator: The Support Vector Machine led Alex and Pythona on a journey through the mathematical landscapes, finding the hyperplane that best separated the data.

Pythona: "Our journey doesn't end here. Birds of a feather flock together, and so do the K-Nearest Neighbors. Import 'KNeighborsRegressor' from sklearn.neighbors, fit the model, and explore the neighborhood of predictions."

Alex: (excited) "K-Nearest Neighbors, welcome! Show us the neighborhood of predictions. Fit, predict, and let the neighbors gather."

Narrator: The K-Nearest Neighbors model gathered predictions from its nearby data points, showcasing the idea that similar instances often share similar outcomes.

Pythona: *"Our exploration of the Model Landscape has been enlightening. Random Forests collaborate, Support Vector Machines find hyperplanes, and K-Nearest Neighbors explore neighborhoods. The summit of algorithms is vast, and our journey continues in the next chapter. Stay tuned for more discoveries!"*

To be continued...

Chapter 8:

The Validation Waltz

Setting: *The Validation Hall, where Alex and Pythona engage in the dance of model validation, exploring Train-Test Split, Cross-Validation, and the graceful Grid Search.*

Narrator: *In the Validation Hall, where models and data engaged in a delicate dance, Alex and Pythona prepared to waltz through the steps of model validation.*

Alex: *(holding a dataset) "Let's start with the Train-Test Split, Pythona. A classic move to ensure our models can dance with new data."*

Pythona: *(gracefully) "Import 'train_test_split' from sklearn.model_selection. Split the dataset into partners - training and testing sets. This way, our model can practice with a partner and perform with a new one."*

Alex: *(performing the split)* "A perfect duet! Now, Cross-Validation, the art of learning from every step. How do we master this dance?"

Pythona: "Summon 'cross_val_score' from sklearn.model_selection. Choose your model, your dataset, and let the dance begin. Cross-Validation ensures our model learns from various partners, making it a versatile dancer."

Narrator: As Alex and Pythona embraced the dance of Cross-Validation, their model twirled gracefully, learning from different perspectives.

Alex: *(curious)* "What about Grid Search, Pythona? How does it refine our model's footwork?"

Pythona: *(revealing the magic)* "Grid Search, the dance of finding the optimal footwork. Import 'GridSearchCV' from sklearn.model_selection. Define the hyperparameter grid, and let Grid Search explore the possibilities, guiding our model to perfection."

Alex: (excited) "Optimizing hyperparameters, a dance of precision! Let's code the Grid Search and witness our model's refined performance."

Narrator: The Validation Hall echoed with the footsteps of the Validation Waltz - Train-Test Split, Cross-Validation, and Grid Search, each contributing to the mastery of model performance.

Pythona: "Our model has danced through validation, learned from every step, and refined its footwork with Grid Search. The Validation Waltz ensures our model is ready for the grand stage of predictions."

Alex: (closing the chapter) "Indeed, Pythona. The dance of validation is a crucial part of our machine learning journey. As we bid farewell to the Validation Hall, the next chapter awaits - a symphony of metrics and insights!"

To be continued...

Chapter 9:

The Clustering Chronicles

Setting: *The Unsupervised Enclave, where Alex and Pythona delve into the enchanting world of Unsupervised Learning, exploring K-Means and Hierarchical Clustering.*

Narrator: *In the Unsupervised Enclave, where mysteries awaited discovery, Alex and Pythona embarked on a tale of clustering. Unsupervised Learning unfolded its magical pages, revealing the stories of K-Means and Hierarchical Clustering.*

Alex: *(with intrigue) "Unsupervised Learning, Pythona. A realm of untold stories where the data reveals its secrets. What tales do K-Means and Hierarchical Clustering have for us?"*

Pythona: *(mystically) "Unsupervised Learning, the art of letting the data guide us. K-Means, a quest for centers. Summon 'KMeans' from sklearn.cluster, and the algorithm will journey through data, seeking clusters and their central tales."*

Alex: *(joining the quest)* "A quest for centers! How does K-Means unfold its tale, Pythona?"

Pythona: "Invoke the 'fit_predict' method on your data, and K-Means will assign each point to the nearest center, creating clusters. The tale reveals itself as patterns emerge, and data finds its own harmony."

Narrator: As K-Means ventured through the data landscape, clusters materialized, each telling a unique story, a harmony of data points finding their companions.

Alex: *(curious)* "And what about Hierarchical Clustering, Pythona? How does it weave the family tree of data?"

Pythona: *(unveiling the scrolls)* "Hierarchical Clustering, the weaver of family trees. Use 'linkage' from scipy.cluster.hierarchy to craft dendrograms. The data's lineage is unveiled, branches forming, and clusters joining hands in a family tree of patterns."

Alex: *(captivated)* "A family tree of data! The branches, the connections, each telling a tale of relationships. Let's explore this mystic world of Hierarchical Clustering."

Narrator: *In the Unsupervised Enclave, K-Means and Hierarchical Clustering revealed the magic of unsupervised tales. Each cluster, each branch in the family tree, whispered secrets of patterns and connections.*

Pythona: "Unsupervised Learning, a tapestry of discovery. K-Means and Hierarchical Clustering, the storytellers, unfold the mysteries of data. Our journey into the Clustering Chronicles has just begun."

Alex: *(closing the chapter)* "Indeed, Pythona. The Unsupervised Enclave has gifted us with the magic of clustering. As we step out, the next chapter beckons - a voyage through metrics, unveiling the measures of our models' tales."

To be continued...

Chapter 10:

The Deep Learning Saga

Setting: *The Neural Haven, where Alex and Pythona venture into the depths of Neural Networks, explore the symphony of Keras, and unravel the visual tales of Convolutional Neural Networks (CNNs).*

Narrator: *In the Neural Haven, where the air hummed with the whispers of neurons, Alex and Pythona embarked on the Deep Learning Saga. The story unfolded with the introduction of Neural Networks.*

Alex: *(in awe) "Neural Networks, Pythona. The very essence of deep learning. How do we dive into this sea of interconnected neurons?"*

Pythona: *(with wisdom) "Neural Networks, the architects of learning. In sklearn, we summon 'MLPClassifier' for classification or 'MLPRegressor' for regression. The layers of neurons intertwine, learning patterns from the data."*

Narrator: *As the Neural Networks awakened, layers of neurons connected, learning intricate patterns, and unveiling the tales encrypted in the data.*

Alex: *(curious) "And what about Keras, Pythona? I've heard it's a symphony of deep learning. How can we compose our own masterpiece?"*

Pythona: *(with a sparkle) "Keras, the maestro of deep learning symphonies. Summon it with 'keras.models.Sequential.' Compose your layers with 'Dense' and let the 'compile' method set the stage. Train your symphony with 'fit.'"*

Narrator: *The symphony of Keras echoed in the Neural Haven as Alex and Pythona composed their masterpiece, the layers harmonizing in the dance of learning.*

Alex: *(peering into the abyss) "And what about Convolutional Neural Networks, Pythona? I've heard they speak the language of images."*

Pythona: (unveiling the scrolls) "Convolutional Neural Networks, the visual poets. Summon 'Conv2D' for convolutional layers. As images speak louder, let the layers capture intricate details, unveiling the visual tales within."

Narrator: In the Neural Haven, CNNs unfolded visual sagas, recognizing patterns and details in the language of images.

Alex: (enthralled) "A symphony of layers, a dance of neurons, and the language of images. The Deep Learning Saga is an enchanting journey. What mysteries await us next, Pythona?"

Pythona: "The deep learning odyssey continues, Alex. The next chapter beckons, where we explore Recurrent Neural Networks and the art of sequence learning."

Narrator: In the Neural Haven, the Deep Learning Saga echoed with the whispers of neurons and the visual poetry of CNNs. The odyssey into the depths of deep learning had only just begun.

To be continued...

Chapter 11:

The Grand Finale

Setting: *The Model Arena, where Alex and Pythona prepare for the Grand Finale, exploring the intricacies of Model Evaluation Metrics, dancing with the pitfalls of Overfitting and Underfitting, and finally, rehearsing for the live performance of Deploying Models.*

Narrator: *In the Model Arena, where models awaited their grand performance, Alex and Pythona prepared for the Grand Finale.*

Alex: *(eager)* "Model Evaluation Metrics, Pythona. The applause or critique after the performance. How do we bow to accuracy, precision, and recall?"

Pythona: *(with flair)* "Model Evaluation Metrics, the judges of our models' performance. Summon them with 'accuracy_score,' 'precision_score,' and 'recall_score.' Let each metric judge the nuances of our models' acts."

Narrator: *The Model Arena resonated with the applause of metrics as Alex and Pythona bowed to accuracy, precision, and recall.*

Alex: *(cautious)* "And what about the twin specters of Overfitting and Underfitting, Pythona? How do we navigate these treacherous traps of the performance stage?"

Pythona: *(revealing the secret scrolls)* "Overfitting and Underfitting, the twin dancers of model performance. Watch for their subtle moves. Use 'validation_curve' and 'learning_curve' to unveil their dance. Find the sweet spot where models shine."

Narrator: In the Model Arena, Alex and Pythona danced with the twin specters, understanding the delicate moves of Overfitting and Underfitting.

Alex: *(anticipating the grand moment)* "And now, Pythona, the climax of our journey – Deploying Models. From the rehearsal stage to the live performance. How do we make our models shine on the grand stage?"

Pythona: *(unveiling the final act)* "Deploying Models, the grand performance. Save your model with 'joblib' or 'pickle.' Rehearse in a local environment, then move to the live stage – be it a website, a mobile app, or the cloud. Let your models shine in the spotlight."

Narrator: *The Model Arena buzzed with the final preparations as Alex and Pythona rehearsed the deployment act, ready to unveil their models on the live stage.*

Alex: *(reflective)* "What a journey it has been, Pythona. From the basics to the grand finale. Our models are ready for the live performance. What a thrilling odyssey!"

Pythona: "Indeed, Alex. The Grand Finale is both an end and a beginning. Our models are set to embark on their journey into the real world, ready to make a difference."

Narrator: *As the curtain fell in the Model Arena, the Grand Finale concluded, leaving the echoes of metrics, the dance of Overfitting and Underfitting, and the anticipation of live deployments lingering in the air.*

To be continued...

Chapter 12:

Epilogue

Setting: *The Enchanted Library, where Alex and Pythona reflect on the Future of Scikit-Learn, continue their Machine Learning Odyssey, and express gratitude in the Acknowledgments.*

Narrator: *In the hallowed halls of the Enchanted Library, Alex and Pythona, having completed their odyssey, gathered for a reflective conversation.*

Alex: *(gazing into the future)* *"The Future of Scikit-Learn, Pythona. What lies ahead in this ever-evolving world of machine learning?"*

Pythona: *(with a knowing smile)* *"The Future of Scikit-Learn, an enchanted realm of possibilities. New algorithms, enhanced features, and a growing community. Let's keep our notebooks open, for the odyssey continues."*

Narrator: *The Enchanted Library echoed with the whispers of algorithms yet to be discovered, and the pages of notebooks waiting to be filled.*

Alex: *(curious)* "And our Machine Learning Odyssey, Pythona? Does it ever truly end?"

Pythona: *(wise)* "The Machine Learning Odyssey, a perpetual journey. With each dataset explored, with every model crafted, the odyssey marches on. Embrace the challenges, savor the victories, and let the odyssey shape the machine learning lore."

Narrator: The Enchanted Library became a haven of knowledge, where the odyssey of machine learning was celebrated as an ongoing saga.

Alex: *(grateful)* "Before we close this enchanting chapter, Pythona, let's express our gratitude. Acknowledgments to those who paved the way and the references that guided us."

Pythona: *(opening a magical scroll)* "Acknowledgments, the tribute to mentors, peers, and the community. Gratitude for the insights shared, the challenges conquered, and the wisdom bestowed upon our journey. And references, the compass that guided us through the vast sea of knowledge."

Narrator: *The Enchanted Library shimmered with gratitude, as Alex and Pythona penned their acknowledgments and references, immortalizing the names that fueled their odyssey.*

Alex: *(closing the enchanted tome)* "And so, Pythona, as we conclude this enchanting tale, may the future be filled with new chapters, new discoveries, and the unwavering spirit of curiosity."

Pythona: *(closing the circle)* "Indeed, Alex. The odyssey is a song that never fades. May the algorithms dance, the notebooks sing, and the machine learning lore continue to unfold."

Narrator: *The Enchanted Library stood as a testament to the journey – an odyssey completed, yet forever ongoing.*

To be continued...

Appendix:

The Script of Code

In this appendix, we present the script of code – the snippets and examples that unfolded in each chapter of our enchanting journey through the world of scikit-learn.

Chapter 1: The Odyssey Begins

Setting: The coding chamber where Alex, Pythona, and the ensemble of algorithms make their first appearance.

Introduction to Machine Learning

from sklearn.model_selection import train_test_split

from sklearn.datasets import load_iris

Load Iris dataset

iris = load_iris()

X_train, X_test, y_train, y_test = train_test_split(iris.data, iris.target, test_size=0.2)

Setting: The ensemble gathers for a collaborative coding session.

Random Forests and Decision Trees

from sklearn.ensemble import RandomForestClassifier

from sklearn.tree import DecisionTreeClassifier

Create Decision Tree and Random Forest models

dt_model = DecisionTreeClassifier()

rf_model = RandomForestClassifier()

Setting: Alex and Pythona prepare their coding environment.

Setting Up Your Environment

import numpy as np

import pandas as pd

import matplotlib.pyplot as plt

import seaborn as sns

Setting: The stage is set for dataset exploration.

Famous Faces: Iris Dataset

iris_df = pd.DataFrame(iris.data, columns=iris.feature_names)

print(iris_df.head())

Chapter 5: The Dance of Preprocessing

Setting: The characters clean the stage and prepare for preprocessing.

Cleaning the Stage: Handling Missing Data

df.dropna(inplace=True)

Feature Scaling and Normalization

from sklearn.preprocessing import StandardScaler

scaler = StandardScaler()

scaled_data = scaler.fit_transform(df[['feature1', 'feature2']])

Setting: Alex and Pythona embark on supervised learning.

Linear Regression

from sklearn.linear_model import LinearRegression

lr_model = LinearRegression()

lr_model.fit(X_train, y_train)

Setting: The ensemble explores Random Forests and Support Vector Machines.

Random Forests

rf_model.fit(X_train, y_train)

Support Vector Machines

from sklearn.svm import SVC

svm_model = SVC()

svm_model.fit(X_train, y_train)

Setting: The ensemble learns the art of validation.

Train-Test Split

X_train, X_test, y_train, y_test = train_test_split(X, y, test_size=0.2)

Cross-Validation

from sklearn.model_selection import cross_val_score

cv_scores = cross_val_score(lr_model, X, y, cv=5)

Setting: The journey into unsupervised learning begins with K-Means.

K-Means Clustering

from sklearn.cluster import KMeans

kmeans_model = KMeans(n_clusters=3)

kmeans_model.fit(X)

Setting: Neural Networks take center stage.

```
# Neural Networks with Keras

from keras.models import Sequential

from keras.layers import Dense


model = Sequential()

model.add(Dense(units=64, activation='relu', input_dim=8))

model.add(Dense(units=1, activation='sigmoid'))
```

Setting: The ensemble evaluates models and prepares for deployment.

Model Evaluation Metrics

from sklearn.metrics import accuracy_score, precision_score, recall_score

y_pred = model.predict(X_test)

accuracy = accuracy_score(y_test, y_pred)

Deploying Models

from joblib import dump

dump(model, 'deployed_model.joblib')

Chapter 12: Epilogue

Setting: The final chapter, where Pythona and Alex reflect on their journey.

The Future of Scikit-Learn

Acknowledgments and References

The Ongoing Machine Learning Odyssey

This concludes our script of code – the magical incantations that brought our machine learning odyssey to life. May your coding adventures be as enchanting as the journey we've shared.

Glossary:

1. **Machine Learning (ML):**

   - *Definition: A field of artificial intelligence (AI) that empowers systems to learn and improve from experience without being explicitly programmed.*

2. **Supervised Learning:**

   - *Definition: A type of ML where the algorithm is trained on a labeled dataset, learning the relationship between input features and corresponding target labels.*

3. **Unsupervised Learning:**

   - *Definition: ML technique where the algorithm is given data without explicit instructions on what to do with it, and it discovers patterns and relationships within the data.*

4. **Feature:**

   - *Definition: An individual measurable property or characteristic of a phenomenon being observed. In ML, features are used to make predictions.*

5. **Label:**

   - *Definition: The output or outcome variable that the model predicts. Also referred to as the target variable.*

6. **Ensemble Learning:**

   - *Definition: A technique where multiple models are combined to improve the overall performance and robustness of the system.*

7. *Decision Tree:*

- *Definition: A tree-like model representing decisions based on conditions. Each node represents a decision based on a feature, leading to branches and leaves with outcomes.*

8. *Random Forest:*

- *Definition: An ensemble learning method that constructs multiple decision trees during training and outputs the mode of the classes.*

9. *Support Vector Machine (SVM):*

- *Definition: A supervised learning algorithm used for classification and regression analysis. It finds the hyperplane that best separates data into classes.*

10. *K-Means Clustering:*

- *Definition: An unsupervised learning algorithm that partitions data into K clusters based on similarity.*

11. *Neural Network:*

- *Definition: A network of interconnected nodes (neurons) inspired by the structure of the human brain. Used for deep learning.*

12. *Keras:*

- *Definition: An open-source deep learning library written in Python. It provides a high-level interface for building neural networks.*

13. *Cross-Validation:*

- *Definition: A technique used to assess how well a model will generalize to an independent dataset by partitioning the data into training and testing sets multiple times.*

14. Grid Search:

- *Definition: A hyperparameter tuning approach that systematically tests a predefined set of hyperparameter combinations to find the best-performing model.*

15. Feature Scaling:

- *Definition: The process of standardizing or normalizing the range of independent variables or features of the dataset.*

16. One-Hot Encoding:

- *Definition: A method of representing categorical variables as binary vectors, where each category is mapped to a distinct binary value.*

17. Label Encoding:

- *Definition: A technique where each label is assigned a unique integer, often used for encoding categorical variables.*

18. Linear Regression:

- *Definition: A linear approach to modeling the relationship between a dependent variable and one or more independent variables.*

19. Mean Squared Error (MSE):

- *Definition: A measure of the average squared difference between predicted and actual values, commonly used for regression problems.*

20. Accuracy:

- *Definition: The ratio of correctly predicted instances to the total instances in a classification problem.*

21. Precision:

- *Definition: The number of true positive predictions divided by the total number of positive predictions.*

22. Recall:

- *Definition: The number of true positive predictions divided by the total number of actual positives.*

23. Deployment:

- *Definition: The process of making a trained machine learning model available for use in real-world applications.*

24. Joblib:

- *Definition: A library in Python that provides tools to provide lightweight pipelining in Python.*

25. Iris Dataset:

- *Definition: A dataset often used for testing machine learning algorithms. It contains measurements of 150 iris flowers from three different species.*

26. Scikit-Learn:

- *Definition: A popular open-source machine learning library in Python, providing simple and efficient tools for data analysis and modeling.*

27. Pandas:

- *Definition: A fast, powerful, and flexible open-source data analysis and manipulation library for Python.*

28. NumPy:

- *Definition: A fundamental package for scientific computing with Python, providing support for large, multi-dimensional arrays and matrices.*

29. Matplotlib:

- *Definition: A comprehensive library for creating static, animated, and interactive visualizations in Python.*

30. Seaborn:

- *Definition: A data visualization library based on Matplotlib that provides a high-level interface for drawing attractive and informative statistical graphics.*

Conclusion:

In conclusion, the journey through the captivating world of scikit-learn has taken us from the basics of machine learning to the deployment of powerful models. This engaging book, written in a dialogue format with lively characters and numerous examples, has aimed to demystify the intricacies of scikit-learn and make the learning experience enjoyable.

Starting with an introduction to machine learning and Python's role in this domain, we met a cast of characters, including Decision Trees, Random Forests, SVMs, K-Means, and more. We explored the ensemble techniques of Bagging and Boosting, and delved into the realm of neural networks, understanding their architecture and significance.

As the plot unfolded, we guided readers through the practical aspects of setting up their environment, installing scikit-learn, and adopting the Pythonic way of importing libraries. We introduced them to famous datasets like Iris, Digits, and Wine, providing a hands-on experience with real-world challenges and opportunities in data exploration.

The dance of preprocessing took center stage as we cleaned the data, explored feature scaling and normalization, and decoded the ciphers of one-hot encoders and label encoders. Crafting the first model involved a gentle start with supervised learning, linear regression, and the art of choices with decision trees.

Navigating the model landscape, we discovered the collaborative ensemble of Random Forests, the hyperplane-seeking SVMs, and the intuitive K-Nearest Neighbors. The validation waltz followed, with techniques like train-test split, cross-validation, and grid search to find the optimal footwork for model evaluation.

The clustering chronicles unveiled the world of unsupervised learning, where K-Means embarked on a quest for centers, and hierarchical clustering created a family tree of patterns. The deep learning saga unfolded with an introduction to neural networks, a symphony of deep learning in Keras, and the image-centric Convolutional Neural Networks (CNNs).

The grand finale showcased the importance of model evaluation metrics, the perils of overfitting and underfitting, and the journey from rehearsal to the live performance of deploying models. In the epilogue, we glimpsed into the future of scikit-learn and reflected on the ongoing machine learning odyssey, expressing gratitude in acknowledgments and references.

The book also provides an appendix with the script of code, offering readers a practical reference for code snippets and examples from each chapter. It is our hope that this engaging and informative journey through scikit-learn has empowered readers with the knowledge and skills to confidently navigate the exciting field of machine learning. As the curtain falls, the future of machine learning awaits, and the adventure continues.

References:

In creating this engaging and informative book on scikit-learn, I drew inspiration and information from various sources. Here is a list of references that have contributed to the development of the content:

1. **"Introduction to Machine Learning with Python: A Guide for Data Scientists"** by Andreas C. Müller and Sarah Guido - This book provided valuable insights into scikit-learn and its applications, serving as a foundational reference for the book's content.

2. **Scikit-Learn Documentation** - The official documentation of scikit-learn was a crucial resource for understanding the intricacies of the library, and it served as a reference for code examples and best practices.

3. **"Python Machine Learning"** by Sebastian Raschka - Sebastian Raschka's book on Python Machine Learning offered additional perspectives on machine learning concepts and scikit-learn usage, enriching the content with practical examples.

4. **Online Learning Platforms** - Various online platforms such as Coursera, Udacity, and Khan Academy have been instrumental in providing insights into machine learning concepts. The knowledge gained from these platforms influenced the content development.

5. **Research Papers and Journals** - Several research papers and journals, especially those related to specific machine learning algorithms and techniques, provided deeper insights and real-world applications.

6. **Community Forums and Discussions** - Engaging with online forums like Stack Overflow and participating in discussions on platforms like GitHub and Kaggle helped in understanding common issues, best practices, and emerging trends in the field.

7. ***Personal Experience and Experimentation*** - *Practical experience in working with machine learning projects and experimenting with scikit-learn played a significant role in shaping the content, ensuring its relevance and applicability.*

8. ***Streamlit Documentation*** - *For the development of the Streamlit application in the final chapters, the official Streamlit documentation was a valuable resource.*

It's important to note that while the characters and dialogues in the book are fictional, the technical content is based on real-world applications and best practices within the field of machine learning. The combination of these resources aimed to provide readers with a comprehensive and engaging learning experience.

KeyTerms:

1. **Machine Learning (ML):** *A field of artificial intelligence (AI) that focuses on developing algorithms and models that enable computers to learn patterns and make predictions or decisions without being explicitly programmed.*

2. **Supervised Learning:** *A type of machine learning where the model is trained on a labeled dataset, meaning that the input data is paired with corresponding output labels.*

3. **Unsupervised Learning:** *A type of machine learning where the model is not provided with labeled output data during training, and it must find patterns or relationships within the input data.*

4. **Scikit-Learn:** *An open-source machine learning library for the Python programming language, providing simple and efficient tools for data analysis and modeling.*

5. **Feature:** *An individual measurable property or characteristic of a phenomenon being observed.*

In machine learning, features are the variables used to make predictions.

6. **Algorithm:** *A set of rules or procedures followed by a computer to solve a problem. In machine learning, algorithms are used to train models on data.*

7. **Model:** *A representation of a real-world process or system that is created by a machine learning algorithm. The model makes predictions based on the patterns it learned during training.*

8. **Cross-Validation:** *A technique used to assess the performance of a machine learning model by splitting the dataset into multiple subsets, training the model on some, and evaluating it on others.*

9. **Overfitting:** *When a machine learning model learns the training data too well, including its noise and outliers, but fails to generalize well to new, unseen data.*

10. **Underfitting:** *When a machine learning model is too simple to capture the underlying patterns in the training data, resulting in poor performance on both training and new data.*

11. **Ensemble Learning:** *A technique that combines the predictions of multiple models to improve overall performance and accuracy.*

12. **Hyperparameter:** *A configuration setting external to the model that can be tuned to optimize the model's performance.*

13. **Feature Scaling:** *The process of standardizing or normalizing the range of independent variables or features of the dataset.*

14. **Clustering:** *A type of unsupervised learning where the goal is to group similar data points together based on certain features.*

15. **Gradient Descent:** *An optimization algorithm used to minimize the error or loss function by adjusting the model's parameters iteratively.*

16. **Neural Network:** *A computational model inspired by the structure and function of the human brain, used for complex pattern recognition tasks.*

17. **Precision and Recall:** *Metrics used to evaluate the performance of a classification model, especially in imbalanced datasets.*

18.   **Random Forest:** An ensemble learning method that constructs multiple decision trees during training and outputs the mode of the classes for classification tasks.

19.   **Support Vector Machine (SVM):** A supervised learning algorithm used for classification and regression analysis that finds the hyperplane that best divides a dataset into classes.

20.   **K-Means Clustering:** A popular clustering algorithm that partitions a dataset into k distinct, non-overlapping subsets (clusters).

Understanding these key terms is essential for navigating the world of machine learning and effectively using scikit-learn for building models.

www.ingramcontent.com/pod-product-compliance
Lightning Source LLC
LaVergne TN
LVHW051537050326
832903LV00033B/4291